'CAUSE I'M THE MOMMY
(THAT'S WHY)!

Happy Mother's Day!

Enjoy!

Love,
Laurie

'97

Lysbeth Guillorn, Editor and Desktop Publisher

Laura Bloch, Cover Design and Design Consultation

Cartoons by Nicole Hollander, reprinted with permission

Cover Photo: Superstock

ISBN 0-96292162-9-3

Printed in the U.S.A. on recycled paper.

HYSTERIA PUBLICATIONS

is a book and calendar publisher dedicated to humor. We are always seeking humorous essays, cartoons and poetry. Please send submissions to:

HYSTERIA PUBLICATIONS
Box 8581, Brewster Station
Bridgeport, CT 06605

Please include SASE and phone number with all submissions and allow six weeks for a reply.

Dedication

"Because of my mother
it never occurred to me
that you couldn't do
what you wanted to do."
— Francine Prose

I dedicate this book to my mom.

Acknowledgments

I wish to acknowledge Don Black for his enthusiastic efforts in helping me to achieve motherhood and for being such a great teammate in the raising of our two greatest collaborations.

I wish to thank my daughters, the two sources of inspiration for all of my stories.

I wish to thank Deb Werksman for her relentless pursuit of excellence as my editor and her nurturing encouragement as my friend.

Contents

Missing Instructions 13
A Lifetime of Support 17
I Am "Womom," Hear Me Roar 21
First-Time Mother 25
The Best Years of My Life 29
A Slice of Heaven 33
No Time for Math 37
Best Supporting Role 41
Two Jobs in a Pod 45
Color Me Baby 51
Truth and the Consequences 55
Sizzling 59
In Disguise 63
Toddling After Fashion 65
Never Look a Gift Crab in the Mouth 69
My Fantasy Dinner 75
A Bite of the American Dream 79
Lonely Trips to the Bathroom 83
A Mother's Resumé 87

CHAPTER 1

MISSING INSTRUCTIONS

Two things I could not get enough of throughout my pregnancy were salt-laden potato chips and instructions on how to prepare for labor. I cannot begin to guess the number of pre-child nights spent munching fried crisps of some kind and leaving greasy fingerprints on book after book by expert after expert, all written to teach me how to make the most of the birth experience.

So when I "went" into labor (they always make it sound like you have to go somewhere to begin contractions), was I scared? No, not at all. For I had become an educated consumer (of both potato chips and anything related to the birth process). Thus, armed with my new-found knowledge (and a can of Pringles just in case), I headed to the hospital in great anticipation of the coming event.

Overall, the experts gave good advice concerning labor and delivery. But, as a result of my own experience, I must say they forgot to mention two very important instructions.

Number One: Do *not* make friends with the hospital staff you meet while walking around prior to delivering your child.

To help my labor progress, the doctor told me to get up and walk, so I did. I think I covered the entire square footage of the hospital. Each time I passed a nurses' station, I would stop and chat for a few moments. They were so friendly. Many of them gave me little tours of their areas and I was just having a great time until ... my water broke. All over brand new (and I hoped water-resistant) carpet in a recently remodeled maternity suite. I was horrified. After much assurance that the carpet would be fine and that they were not going to make me clean up the mess (which was great because given my body dimensions at the time, it would have taken an act of God to get me successfully down to floor level), they sent me back to the delivery area. Labor progressed, and after what seemed like hours of pushing with my head down and eyes closed in total concentration, the doctor told me to look up at the mirror in front of me as the baby's head was emerging. I did look up but it was not the mirror that greeted my horrified eyes. Instead, framed by the victory sign of my legs in stirrups, was the group of hospital "friends" I had made earlier. All of them. Clapping and applauding and yes, excitedly pointing at my blushing vagina.

Number Two: Handle gently the technician who comes to take a sample of your blood.

Said technician was behind schedule and I was well into active labor when he arrived. He apologized profusely for the interruption and assured me he would try to be as quick as possible. Unfortunately for him, just as he was putting the needle in my arm, I experienced a contraction that put all others to shame, and instinctively grabbed the closest thing I could find — his arm. I hung on until the contraction was over and then it was my turn to apologize. Grimacing with pain, he told me not to worry. I didn't. In fact, I completely forgot about it until the next day when I was in the elevator heading down to the gift shop.

Of course the elevator was crowded. Of course he had an unbelievably loud voice when he boomed from the back: "Hey! It's you! Wow! You were really wild last night. Look at the scratch marks you left on my arm!"

It was the longest elevator ride of my life...

CHAPTER 2

A LIFETIME OF SUPPORT

Even though I gave birth to one average-sized newborn, my breasts mistakenly thought I was a having a litter. They began tingling in the delivery room soon after my last great push and as I was being wheeled to the maternity floor, they started leaking huge quantities of a clear liquid, later identified as colostrum. Whatever. By the time we made it to my room, I was able to ride in on a wave of my own making where I then landed with a great splash onto the bed. The triumphant first-time giver-of-life resplendent in all her motherly glory?

No, more like one big human puddle surrounded by a head, hands and feet.

"Aren't you lucky," the nurses cooed. "Most new mothers spend the majority of their time worrying about having enough of a supply for their newborns. But you, well, my goodness, you have enough for everyone."

Comforting words? Terrifying words. In my post-delivery, highly emotional state, all I could picture was a horde of other highly emotional but colostrum-deficient new moms tracking me down and frantically trying to grab my nipples to feed their hungry babies.

I was told my "regular" milk would most likely show up around the second or third day post-birth. Unfortunately, my breasts weren't listening and began producing the "real" stuff early the following morning. I watched in disbelief as my breasts swelled and swelled and swelled. They they got warm. Really warm. Hot. In a panic, I managed to reach way around them and push the call button. By the time the nurse arrived, they'd started to turn red and you could actually see the veins throbbing. I didn't know whether to beg the RN for help or tell her to run for cover — I was certain they were gonna blow.

She just chuckled and told me they were engorged (more like *enraged,* to my way of thinking). She told me I needed to express them. I told her I thought they were expressing themselves quite clearly. *They were mad!* She reassured me that all would be well once I had the baby nursing. On her way to get my newborn, she told me to use my hand to pump out some milk so that my daughter would be able to latch onto a nipple. I began pumping and finally felt a little less overwhelmed as I had a nice, manageable stream from both nipples and my breasts were beginning to feel oh so much better.

As soon as my daughter was in the room and crying, those nice little streams turned immediately into roaring rivers cascading down my chest, down the bed, out the door...

So you can imagine what happened when I attempted to place my newborn's tiny, heart-shaped mouth over one of my raging faucets. She looked a little like one of those courageous salmon swimming upstream bravely, but hopelessly, against the current. After a second or two, she started howling and so did I. It took a while before the nurse could calm us both down (and dry us off) but when she did, she assured me that within just a few days, my flow would adjust to my infant's needs and everyone would be happy.

Just as the nurse predicted, my flow did slow down and adjust to my child's needs and thus, my daughter was quite content and would have liked nothing better than to suckle leisurely at my breasts from dawn to dusk. Which was fine with me. That is, until my nipples decided to go on the warpath. I never thought it possible that two small little buds of flesh could be capable of generating so much pain. When I called the doctor's office describing my raw and cracked tips, the nurse asked if I had done any nipple toughening exercises while pregnant. Nipple toughening exercises? The only exercising I did while enceinte was the lifting of my hand, holding some tasty, fat-filled morsel to my mouth.

Fortunately, after a week or so of applying lanolin and heat after every feeding along with walking around topless so that they could air-dry (the UPS man didn't seem to mind), my nipples healed and the four of us: me, my breasts, and my newborn, finally bonded and thoroughly enjoyed our time together.

And even though we got off to a bit of a rocky start, in return for hanging in there and helping my child begin her life in the most nutritious way possible, I have promised my breasts a lifetime of support.

CHAPTER 3

I AM "WOMOM," HEAR ME ROAR

My friends contemplating motherhood often ask what it's really like to go from being a "woman" to a "womom." I've tried to come up with detailed explanations of the lifestyle changes but feel the following examples say it best:

A "woman," surrounding herself in candlelight and fragrant bubbles, takes a sip from her glass of favorite wine as she sinks ever so slowly into the welcoming liquid heat. Closing her eyes, she completely relaxes as the steamy bathwater gently laps away the day's worries.

A "womom" sinks into the bath ever so slowly because of the kid-skid resistant pad now covering the entire length of the tub. Closing her eyes, fully enjoying the complete and utter silence of finally being alone, she suddenly feels she's being watched. Eyes snapping open, she finds herself face to face with a floating Big Bird and his merry band of waterproof muppets.

•

A "woman" prepares for a weekend getaway by packing an overnight bag.

A "womom" prepares for a weekend getaway by packing a small U-Haul truck.

•

A "woman" sharing her bed snuggles lovingly with her partner as he whispers sweet nothings in her ear.

A "womom" sharing her bed attempts to snuggle with her partner but finds a couple of little people in the way. Instead of hearing sweet nothings in her ear, she hears a tiny voice whispering an apology just as the bed sheets become noticeably and uncomfortably wet — again.

•

A "woman" bases what she's going to fix for dinner on the type of mood she's in and how hungry she's feeling.

A "womom" bases what she's going to fix for dinner on the type of food that is most easily removed from kitchen walls, chairs and hair.

•

A "woman" can recite the Pledge of Allegiance and the Lord's Prayer.

A "womom" can recite the Pledge of Allegiance, the

Lord's Prayer and all the words to the "Barney's a Dinosaur" theme song.

•

A "woman" stops to smell the roses.

A "womom" stops to try and pull the roses out of her child's mouth.

•

A "woman" is a wondrous creature of great intelligence, a marvelous wit, and the ability to find goodness in almost every situation.

A "womom" is a wondrous creature filled with great intelligence, a marvelous wit, the ability to find goodness in almost every situation, and the awesome responsibility of raising another human being. Although there are moments when being a mother brings forth feelings of frustration and even helplessness, there are many, many more moments when being a mother brings on feelings of a love so unselfish it almost overwhelms the soul.

SYLVIA by Nicole Hollander

CHAPTER 4

FIRST-TIME MOTHER

Being a first-time mother is one of the scariest experiences I've lived through. I remember crying big, Texas-sized tears of terror as my favorite nurse turned traitor on me and sent for the wheelchair that would roll me and my firstborn away from the safety net of the hospital and into the frightening "real" world.

At home there would be no magic blue button by my bedside to be pushed whenever I needed a fairy godnurse to appear.

Of course I always knew that we'd eventually be leaving the hospital, but I was just too busy basking in the glory of my latest creation, surrounded by gorgeous flowers and adoring relatives, to actually concern myself with the realities of caring for a newborn minus a staff of nurses. I suppose in my new-mother euphoria, I just assumed that along with my complimentary carseat, bottles of sugar water and episiotomy numbing spray, I'd also get to choose a complimentary nurse to come live with us, say, for the first year or so.

Bad assumption on my part.

How was the first night home? Looking back on it, I'm hard pressed to remember who cried the loudest or the longest. I cried because I felt so utterly incompetent as a mother. The baby cried because she was probably wondering how she'd ended up with someone who obviously didn't know the first thing about newborns.

My husband cried because he had to go to work in the morning and wasn't getting any sleep. Our dog cried, because this tiny, new, squalling thing with no hair, wrinkled skin, and a mottled red face meant he'd just become an outdoor pet.

So I read. Voraciously. If a book bore the names of T. Berry Brazelton or Penelope Leach, I grabbed it. Like many a superior student who excels in the classroom and flounders in the real world, I found that even though I could recite how to "bathe, burp, diaper and dress" an infant, my own attempts at performing these activities were mediocre at best. And although we'd done okay at breastfeeding while in the hospital, being at home was a completely different matter.

In desperation, I phoned my pediatrician. After all, hadn't he kindly told me it was okay to call day or night, anytime I had an emergency? Well, this was definitely an emergency. My baby girl was obviously going to starve to death because she'd only nurse on my breast for about two minutes before falling soundly asleep. The experts had stated quite clearly that all babies needed to nurse at least *ten* minutes. After explaining that this was not exactly the type of emergency that required a 2 a.m. call, the doctor (God bless him for not hanging up on me) soothingly suggested that I get a cool washrag and lightly rub the soles of my daughter's feet to wake her up. I wrote down his directions word for word, got my cold washrag and started to rub when I realized I had forgotten to ask some very important questions: How hard was I supposed to rub? Her skin was already peeling quite a bit, most noticeably around her feet, and I certainly didn't want to accidently rub her raw all the way down to her heel bones. And exactly how long was I supposed to rub? If I rubbed too long, couldn't she catch pneumonia from all that cold water being absorbed through her feet where it would eventually wind up, say, in her lungs?

Time passed, and amazingly enough, my newborn did not starve. She also never experienced "exposure of the heel bones" nor did she catch pneumonia due to wet feet. In fact as time went by, I actually managed to go an hour or two without worrying that she'd bleed to death due to a fingernail being cut too close to the quick, that she'd slide out of my arms and down the kitchen drain as I bathed her or that the nipple from her bottle would suddenly loosen and escape down her throat.

There were even moments when she and I would gaze deeply into one another's eyes and know we were survivors — me, as a first-time mother, and she, as a daughter surviving me, as a first-time mother.

SYLVIA by Nicole Hollander

CHAPTER 5

THE BEST YEARS OF MY LIFE

If you're like me, you are constantly being reminded (always by people whose children are grown) that these years (when the children are small) will be the best years of your life.

So when I leave my three-year-old and her friend happily swinging outside for *two minutes* while I run inside to get them snacks, I find myself in a state of shock when I walk back out the door. There the little darlings are, no longer on swings, but instead, busily scooping up dog poop from the designated "dumping" ground behind the garden into the brand new sandbox filled with fresh sand. Taking a deep breath and wondering how I'm going to explain to the friend's mother why her daughter has such an "interesting fragrance" about her, I have to try really hard to remember that these are the best years of my life...

Or when I have just finished an hour of play with my twelve-month-old and I decide she can play with one of her millions of toys by herself while I jot down ideas on my notebook computer, she decides the only activity she wants to do is walk across my keyboard. She loves the clicking sound it makes, and when she's done she sits down to lick the keys while I wonder if all that saliva is going to short-circuit the computer. And as I sit there with my soggy keyboard, I have to try really, really hard to remember that these are the best years of my life...

Or just after letting my oldest choose a coloring book from the toy aisle while at the grocery store, we are waiting in the checkout line and she spots a Mickey Mouse balloon that she can't live without. First I try the "experts'"approach of patiently explaining why (people in line are nodding approvingly at my calm approach) but unfortunately, while everyone else understands that a Mickey Mouse face filled with hot air won't guarantee a lifetime of happiness, my daughter is now screaming that she must have the baloon. Fed up with her tantrum, I tell her in my "mean mother/ wicked witch of the east" voice that not only is she *not* going to get the baloon, but if she doesn't be quiet, she can look forward to a full day in one of the numerous "time out" corners in our home. Her response is to look her most innocent and tell me in a soft, sweet voice to "please, please be nicer to me." And then she starts to whimper, which sets my youngest off because she feels compelled to mirror whatever emotion her big sister is displaying. Naturally, with both of my children in tears, those same "other people" in line who were impressed with my initial calm demeanor are now silently condemning me with their "wicked witch of the east" eyes for making two such obviously sweet young children cry. It's at this point that I have to try really, really, really hard to remember that these are the best years of my life...

Groceries loaded, we start home, and by the time I pull into the driveway the girls are fast asleep, holding hands across the distance between their seats. They look like two little angels in sweet repose. Silently thanking God for finally giving me a moment's peace, I suddenly experience a revelation that leaves me with the knowledge of why these are, indeed, the best years of my life: because if I can survive them, they will surely guarantee me a first-class ticket into heaven.

CHAPTER 6

A SLICE OF HEAVEN

My husband asked the other night what I do while our two daughters are at "Mother's Day Out." My explanation surprised him a bit, but for mothers with preschoolers, my response might sound quite heavenly.

After dropping the kids off, the first thing I do is head home and pour myself a glass of "something." It's not important to me what the "something" is, and oftentimes I'm not really even very thirsty. So why do it? Because I know that when I fix this beverage, *it's all mine!* I don't have to share even a sip of it with grubby little people who leave sticky handprints on the outside of the glass and bits and pieces of whatever they happened to have in their mouths floating on the inside. No siree — it's mine and mine alone, to enjoy at leisure. Sometimes, I'll just sit for hours "drinking in" the beauty of a clean glass filled with clear liquid.

Next on the list is a bath. It doesn't matter if I've already soaped up earlier in the day, because cleanliness is not the objective. What's really important is that I get to enjoy reclining in a tub filled to the brim with nothing more than sudsy, scented bubblebath and hot, steamy water. No toy boats, swimming Barbie dolls or alphabet letters that stick to the sides. Better yet, the only hands available to wash me, if I so desire, are my own. No tiny out-of-control fingers sticking Pooh Bear soap in my hair, in my eyes or up my nose. Just me, the bubbles and a good-sized stack of catalogs to meander through without anyone grabbing them, tearing them or eating the pages.

Following my bath is the last activity I indulge in before picking up the kids. I call it "free driving," and all that's required is leaving the house at least an hour or so before school lets out. Their school is only minutes from my house, but being the sole occupant of a vehicle for just under an hour has become for me like a slice of heaven. To begin with, instead of listening to the Lion King tape for the zillionth time, I, as the only passenger, get to choose a radio station where the songs are sung by people and not lions, warthogs, strange little birds and hyenas. Happily humming with the music, I then get to experience "schedule-free" independence. This means at least forty-five minutes of driving simply for the sheer pleasure of being behind the wheel with absolutely no destination in mind. What a wonderful reprieve from the norm — driving at breakneck speed (praying there's a local doughnut convention to keep the police busy) to gymnastics, dance class, art school or some other activity. All these are designed to enrich my children's lives while turning their mother into a crazed chauffeur whose greatest fear is that one activity will inadvertently be overlooked and no make-ups will be allowed.

So there you have it, a description of this mother's "Mother's Day Out." Just taking the golden opportunity to rediscover the pleasures of being all alone with the one person who knows and appreciates me better than anyone else: myself.

by Nicole Hollander

CHAPTER 7

NO TIME FOR MATH

I'd like to do my part to help disprove the old, ridiculous stereotype that says women aren't good with numbers, but quite frankly, I just don't have the time.

Every morning, before my girls are awake, I'm busy in the kitchen getting breakfast ready. Let's see, one egg equals ½ of a four-year-old's stomach, so with a four-and-a-half-year-old and a two-year-old, the total sum of eggs needing to be scrambled equals 3½, so that leaves me with a remainder of ½ of an egg, which will be just enough to top off our dog's daily meal. He weighs 10 pounds which means he gets two cups (one cup for every 5 pounds) and we like to treat him with ¼ of an egg per cup of food.

After breakfast, while the kids go outside to play on the rectangular-shaped hopscotch pad and bounce the circular-shaped basketball on the square-shaped court and, of course, fly their parallelogram-shaped kites across the infinitude of the sky, I'm busy inside mopping the kitchen floor, cleaning the guest bathroom and doing the day's worth of laundry.

Almost by rote, I get the floor cleaner, mix the standard ¼ cup of product with 1 gallon of warm water and plunge the mop into the frothy mixture a good 4 times. Oh sure, I've tried plunging just 2 times but have found 2 times the plunge does not an adequately saturated mop area make.

Next on the list is the bathroom. Remembering my friend's latest beau (a rather grungy fellow, with rings in both nipples and belly, who not only talked for hours about the actual piercings, but graciously offered to show us the puncture marks and wouldn't take no for an answer) and the inordinate number of times he visited the guest bathroom during dinner last night (I noticed he "went" 4 times for a total of 36 minutes, which meant he averaged 9 minutes per trip — what was he doing in there?!), I think a good disinfection session is in order. And I've got to tell you, the disinfectant I prefer has more than proven its "absolute value" to me because it promises to get rid of just about every type of germ (and I have a feeling he left one of each kind behind).

Last on the list of chores is the laundry. But before I attack it, the girls come in, ready for lunch. Both immediately request a hotdog so I naturally get out 4. Yes, you guessed it. The egg formula also applies to hotdogs. The remaining ½ hotdog is usually saved to top off the dog's meal on the morning I realize I've run out of eggs.

But back to the laundry. I've got about 16 pieces of clothing that fit in the "hot water" category, and I know that my washer can comfortably hold up to 10 pieces per load so it looks like a 2-cycle kind of day — gee, I usually do 4 loads a day so it's a nice surprise to find I have to do only 50% of the norm.

Which is good because my friend just called (she broke up with her hole-ridden boyfriend) and wants to come over for dessert, coffee, and a shoulder to cry on. Great, I knew I should have made apple pie squared.

Anyway, you can see why, by the end of the day, I'm just too tired to think about math. Indeed, I want nothing more than to lay my weary head on my rectangular-shaped pillow and count a couple of sets of sheep before falling soundly asleep.

CHAPTER 8

BEST SUPPORTING ROLE

Sure, anyone can get an Oscar in the supporting role category for movies, but I think there is a great need to have a brand new category for a supporting role award. I am calling it "Best Supporting Role in Motherhood" and the nominees are my treasured friends (actually more like support group) who have become a part of my life through my children.

My first nominee is my friend Kris. She is the calm, think-it-through Ethel, to my crazy, full-of-wild-ideas Lucy. But like Ethel she is always a willing partner in crime and has yet to utter "I told you so" when one of my "great" ideas goes awry (like the time I thought it would be a cultural experience for our kids — all five of them under the age of six — to visit a local historical landmark home filled with priceless antiques). She is a fountain of child-related wisdom (having already encountered and survived the toddler years with her oldest son) but never spews out advice uncontrollably as most folks are apt to do. And somehow (God knows how, with three children and a husband who travels all week) she always find the time to listen when I need a sounding board. You know, sometimes I think God decided to give me a break and put my guardian angel here on earth in the form of Kris.

My second nominee is my friend Kimberly. Even though she happens to be gorgeous, she couldn't care less about her looks as she is far too busy having fun with her two boys to waste much time in front of the mirror. If Drew and Reed go digging for earthworms, their mother is right beside them doing her own worm excavation (minus those grown-up sissy garden gloves, of course). If her kids are in a neighborhood softball game, she is in the middle of it, and let me tell you, each team fights to get her on their side. I love being around Kimberly because she reminds me by example how important it is to admire my children and communicate with them on their level. Kimberly teaches me how to be a kid again.

My third nominee is my friend Elizabeth. Elizabeth amazes me with her willingness to help others. She is the friend that shows up on my doorstep with a complete meal in tow when I am sick, she is the friend that offers to help me chauffer my children (even though she is busy with her own) when I have committed myself to being three places at once. And most important, she is the friend that has shown me the importance of making time to help others. Her volunteering covers both ends of the spectrum — she is currently a "big sister" assigned to help a sixteen-year-old girl with a newborn complete her high school education and she also delivers food to the elderly twice a month through the Meals On Wheels program. Elizabeth inspires me and my kids to do something nice for someone else, not because of the glory in recognition we will receive for doing it, but just because it is the right thing to do.

And the winner is...

Me, of course, for having three such wonderful women in my life.

SYLVIA by Nicole Hollander

CHAPTER 9

TWO JOBS IN A POD

Having spent eight years as a computer programmer before becoming a mom, I know a lot about both types of jobs and I am telling you, the commonalities are nothing short of amazing. Who would have guessed? But it's true.

The first similarity I noticed has to do with helping people define realistic expectations.

As a computer programmer, in order to know what type of program needed to be written, I was required to attend "requirements sessions." At these meetings, the end users were supposed to describe what they felt the program had to do for them in terms of capabilities, while I was there to gently (but firmly) help them identify realistic expectations. Unfortunately, the meetings would become rather heated because, when asked what they absolutely had to have within a given timeframe, they would always give the same answer: "We must have a program that does everything we can possibly think of and anything else we might forget to mention."

As a mom, I have a job that also includes helping

people define realistic expectations, the only real difference being that the "people" I meet with are under the age of five. If my kids had their way, we would start the morning at Discovery Zone with a hotdog and Coke for breakfast and then jaunt over to the new McDonald's to romp around the indoor playground and indulge in a midday snack consisting of the always nutritious chocolate milkshake and friench fries combination before zipping over to Chuck E Cheese's to play all the indoor games and "do" lunch with a gooey, Chuck E Cheese pizza. Our final destination would of course, be "Six Flags Over Texas," where we would enjoy a late afternoon, early evening and, hey, what the heck, all-night session of amusement park rides stopping only long enough to down corn dogs, cotton candy and extra-sugary lemonades in between the roller coaster rides.

Another similarity has to do with the idea of action plans. Before I coded a computer program, it was required that I first submit a detailed action plan describing every task involved in creating the computer program and the order in which the tasks would be executed. From this action plan, a timeline would then be developed to show the approximate date of when my program would be ready for public use.

Well, guess what? My life as a full-time mom has become one giant action plan. I have tasks coming out the wazoo. Fix breakfast, pack school lunches, iron school uniforms, locate matching socks, find something from home that begins with whatever alphabet letter my kindergartener is studying, search hopelessly for school backpacks, get kids to school by 8 a.m., race to the gas station and then zoom back to the school just in the nick of time to pick up a group of kids and head out on a field trip, to name just a few of my tasks. Unfortunately, the tasks are currently stored in my head because I simply have not had time to perform the taks of "writing all the tasks down" yet! I also have a timeline that shows an approximate date of when I will be done with this current "project." It will be sometime in the year 2010 when both of my children are in college.

And then there was my worst nightmare as a computer programmer: the dreaded endless loop. The endless loop would occur if I accidentally wrote a program that basically told the computer to keep doing the same thing, well, forever. And the only way one could break out of "forever" would be to turn the computer off (not exactly a user-friendly way of handling things).

Although the environment is a little different, I also experience endless loops as a mother. They usually occur when I ask one of my kids to do something. The endless loop scenario goes something like this:

Me: "Brooke, would you please make your bed?"

Brooke: "Why? I'm going to sleep in it again tonight."

Me: "Brooke, would you please make your bed?"

Brooke: "I don't see why I have to, Shelby and Hailey told me their moms never make them do it."

Me: "Brooke, would you please make your bed?"

Brooke: "You don't love me. I am running away."

Usually an effective way to break out of this type of endless loop is with a time-out. Unfortunately, the solution may also serve as a catalyst to yet another endless loop:

Me: "Enough! You are now in time-out until I say you may get out."

Brooke: "When are you going to say I can get out?"

Me: "You are in time-out until I say you may get out."

Brooke: "It's my right to know when you are going to let me out."

Me: "You are in time-out until I say you may get out!"

Brooke: "You don't love me. I am running away."

I suppose the only 100% effective way of disabling a mother's endless loop like the one described above has to do with the timeline mentioned earlier — something about the year 2010 in my case...

The final similarity to be noted has to do with something both the programmer and mother hope to achieve: Robustness.

When I was a computer programmer, "robustness" meant creating a program that was protected against all possible crashes from bad data and unexpected values (basically meant there was nothing that anyone or anything could do that would have caused my program to fail).

For a mom, "robustness" pretty much follows the same stream of thought as described above except that

I am trying to create future adults that will have in abundance the self-esteem, courage and sense of adventure necessary to protect themselves against the negativity and narrow-mindedness so prevalent in today's world.

I mean, who knows, they just might run into a really unenlightened soul who cannot even see the blatant similarities between, say, the job of a computer programmer and the job of a mother...

by Nicole Hollander

CHAPTER 10

COLOR ME BABY

Sure, I'd like to be a "Color Me Beautiful" gal. You know, a worldly Winter, a spectacular Spring, a shimmering Summer, or an adventurous Autumn, but quite frankly, they have yet to create a season with a palate that will weather my current lifestyle as a mom.

So, it appears I will have to create my own. This should not be too difficult, as I have already identified the appropriate colors for a mother with two very young, very messy children:

First, my "foundation" colors. Well, where would I be without the always radiant squash-orange; the pureed turkey yellow; the strained spinach green; and, of course, the color forever in vogue: milky off-white, or "ecru."

Next would be my "accent" colors. Hmm, I think perhaps plum-based beet purple along with the lovely pea brown streaked with yellow should do the trick.

The colors defined, it is now time to take my newly created palette and "translate" it into a wardrobe consisting of outfits with the "right" combination of colors for each of my activities.

Going to the grocery store. We always go directly after breakfast. It used to be that some wise guy sacker at the checkout stand would point out the splotches of what appeared to be a thick paste of some kind haphazardly spread across my clothing. Embarrassed, I would rush to explain that my shirt and pants, dress, whatever, had started out looking fresh and completely free of splotches but that after breakfast with a two-year-old, it ended up looking less than perfect.

But no more. With my new color palette, standing out from the crowd due to extreme splotchiness will become a thing of the past. From now on, my morning ensemble will consist of one color: ecru. Ecru dress, ecru skirt and matching ecru blouse. Ecru here, ecru there, ecru, ecru, everywhere. This way, when Annie decides to launch her usual milk-laden teaspoon-sized missiles of oatmeal or baby cereal at me, I will not duck. I will stand and enjoy the sound of the splat against my body. And as soon as the splat dries, I will simply brush myself off. And what doesn't brush off will easily blend in with my outfit, and no one, not even a smart alec sacker, will be the wiser.

After lunch, afternoons spent outside romping with the girls is a favorite activity most days. Brooke enjoys rolling in the grass and dirt while her little sister takes great delight in eating the grass and dirt. All would be fine if no one came to our house during this play time. But, alas, they do. And when I answer the door, I am usually looked at in surprise as the guest wonders why I resemble a cross between the jolly green giant and the swamp thing. But no more. I now have the perfect outfit: a strained, spinach green warmup suit with turkey yellow highlights I recently lucked into at a retired army officer's garage sale.

Before we know it, dinnertime rolls around. Because of my husband's job, we do quite a bit of business entertaining. In the past, trying to feed the kids before we went out would turn into a hopeless and frustrating attempt to keep food from lodging itself in my outfit. Desperate for another way to stay clean, I tried dressing after the kids ate. But no matter. Even then, some leftover glop of guaranteed-to-clash food would invariably stick to my silk blouse or expensive dress just as we were escaping out the door.

But with my new wardrobe, that problem is a thing of the past. The key to leaving the house still looking good is a little pre-dinner planning. And all that involves is a quick trip to the closet to choose my outfit followed by a quick trip to the pantry to decide what will "go" with it. For example, if I choose to wear my brown silk jumpsuit accented with an oversized scarf made up of dominant splashes of muted gold, red, and green on it, then the kids will, of course, be eating turkey fingers, mashed beans, and strained spinach, followed by raspberry jello for dessert.

Gosh, I feel so much better knowing that I have finally discovered the right season for me. I have decided to call it "Color Me Baby."

by Nicole Hollander

CHAPTER 11

TRUTH AND THE CONSEQUENCES

I'm constantly amazed how many other names are used when referring to the vagina or the penis. Especially when dealing with children. For example, we were eating dinner with another family at a local restaurant when little Lisa turned to her mom and stated: "Mommy, my she-she needs to go wee-wee." And with the usual chain reaction, her brother piped right in with "Daddy, my he-he needs to go pee-pee." Fortunately, because my two girls had no idea what their friends were talking about, I got to skip the adventure of taking toddlers to a foreign bathroom. On another occasion, while playing at the park, I actually heard a man say to his son who was holding his crotch, "Hey Tim, my man, do ya need to go drain your tool (grunt, grunt)?" I mean, come on — his "tool"?

She-she, he-he and tool? Nope, I decided that when my girls were old enough to ask, they would simply be told the "real" names of the body part and body function in question. So, when my three-and-a-half-year-old pointed below her waist and asked why water came out, I explained it was called a vagina and the "water" was called urine and to please not drink it or try to get her little sister to drink it. And when she happened to see her dad using the bathroom and asked what that "thing" was and why he stood up, I simply told her that "thing" was a penis and that's what men and boys use to urinate (and to please not ever grab it like a rope to swing from ever again)...

For awhile, she'd say "Daddy has a peanut" and, not wanting to have my child accidently create yet another ridiculous slang word for penis (not to mention my husband's embarrassment over being called the man with the peanut), I spent quite a bit of time getting her to pronounce "penis" correctly.

Alas, sometimes complete honesty can backfire, and even though I'm still a firm believer in teaching kids the "real" words for any body part of the body and its function, I'm quite sure our "straight" talk was not appreciated during our most recent journey to Hot Springs Village, Arkansas.

Usually we go there to visit relatives; this time the trip was due to the death of Uncle Tom. We hadn't wanted to bring the kids but Aunt Betty insisted that they would be "rays of sunshine" during an otherwise somber event. It seemed Aunt Betty was right, too — all of the people we met (90% were over the age of 70) seemed to enjoy watching the antics of two little girls. And even during the memorial service, the girls behaved admirably. In fact, by the time the service was over, I was in the blissful and euphoric state of knowing I had two of the best little girls in the world.

Then came the dinner following the memorial service. Because everyone just loved our little darlings (my youngest was blowing kisses to everyone, which was so cuuuuuuuuuutttttte), the table we chose quickly filled with grandmas, grandpas and great-grandparents eagerly wanting to spend more time with our two kids, who probably reminded them of their own grandchildren and great-grandchildren.

So there we all were, my husband and I beaming with pride over our perfect children, waiting to hear what lovable statements the two little angels would make. Well, the oldest angel decided not to waste this moment in the spotlight and with a glance around the entire table, she took a deep breath, began pointing to each of our table mates while saying clearly and loudly (oh, so clearly and loudly): "You have a penis, and you have a vagina, and you have a penis, and..." until all the vaginas and penises at our table had been addressed.

I had never before seen the "domino effect" of mouths dropping open in shock and, quite frankly, I hope never to again. All I could think during those moments of great trial and tribulation (with my husband muttering, "You just had to teach her to say penis correctly, didn't you...") was that at least my littlest angel hadn't let me down. As I bent my head to kiss her silky soft blond halo, I couldn't help but notice — as did everyone else — that she was quite busy with her finger up her nose.

CHAPTER 12

SIZZLING

You've probably noticed all the "add spice to your sex life" articles currently appearing in most magazines. One in particular caught my attention: It described a guaranteed way to make me and my "lovemate" "sizzle" in sexual anticipation.

You see, with two young children running around in circles (which keeps me and their dad running around in circles), there's not a whole lot of time for anything else. And after all that running, any free moments are usually spent resting.

But sizzling sounded like such a red hot idea, I felt I had to give it a try. So I read the article's instructions and learned that, basically, all I had to do was get one tape recording of me and my lovemate fooling around. And if I could tape it without my partner's knowledge, so much the better, for that was supposed to add even more sparks at play back time.

Not usually keen on having anything I do taped, I decided to put aside my misgivings, because, according to the article, once recorded, this cassette would be an instant aphrodisiac guaranteed to take us to new heights of afternoon (or morning, or nighttime) delight simply by playing it!

But before I could play it, I had to tape it, and before I could tape it, I had to dig up a tape recorder. Rummaging through my two-year-old's toy chest, I quickly spotted my treasure: a bright yellow "Big Bird" recorder.

Next on the list was a blank tape. Unfortunately, this turned out to be a bit of a problem. The only cassette I could find held my four-year-old's tap recital song, but after a momentary twinge of guilt I erased it. Sure, we'd all miss hearing "On the Good Ship Lollipop" but to be honest, the choice between listening to Shirley Temple sing about her trip to the candy shop to eat all the sweets that I'm trying so hard to avoid and sizzling in sexual anticipation was not a hard one to make.

Having procured the necessary "pre-sizzle" components, all that was left was the taping. As luck would have it, an opportunity to perform the final deed presented itself on Saturday morning. For as soon as the kids ate their usual breakfast of cereal, toast and bananas dipped in picante sauce (they're both native Texans), two fat little legs wobbled out of the kitchen and into the living room to watch cartoons.

So, as the girls sat entranced with Bugs Bunny, Donald Trump (I mean Duck) and all of their animated buddies, I quickly awakened my nearly asleep spouse, and by mid-morning, both the tape recorder and newly-taped-on cassette were safely hidden under my side of the bed (the only place I knew the kids wouldn't go because that's where monsters live). And although I had been able to keep it a secret from my spouse, I must admit I was really tempted to play it back immediately for myself. But then I remembered the article stressed the listening should be a "together" experience.

Knowing a long night of wining, dining and being "together," wouldn't be possible with two toddlers close by, I called the grandparents. With just minimal begging and my signature on a notarized note promising I'd replace whatever got broken, they agreed to babysit at their house.

The big night arrived and after finishing a lovely meal made even more special because we didn't have to dodge catapulting toddler-sized silverware or spend hours removing odd bits of food from the walls, table and chairs, we retired to the bedroom.

I lit some candles (actually a whole bunch — we had only the small birthday kind) and put on my sexiest T-shirt. Well, okay, it was the same T-shirt I wore every night but at least I didn't accessorize with my usual thermal ankle socks and my face wasn't smeared with its normal glob of anti-aging wonder cream.

Winking seductively at my husband (he asked if I had something in my eye), I retrieved the tape recorder and cassette. While he jokingly asked if we were going to "tap off" our dinner (see, I told you "we'd" all miss the Goodship Lollipop), I snuggled next to my lovemate, told him I had a grand surprise and hit the play button.

As it turns out, there was a heckuva surprise in store for both of us. I suppose we could've sizzled in sexual anticipation but that's tough to do while doubled over in laughter with tears streaming from your eyes. You see, our aphrodisiac recording went something like this:

"Gee, Honey, guess it's been awhile, do you remember how to do this?"

"No, I really don't but I read somewhere that you never forget how to ride a bike so maybe if we got on top of your old ten speed, this would come back as well."

"MMMmmm you smell really good — like strawberry jam — oh, wait a minute, you've got a big glob of it in your hair."

"Great. I was wondering where Annie left her piece of breakfast toast. Do you see any slightly burned bread nearby?"

"Oh no. Did you hear that?"

"Hear what? I found the bread, she stuck it in my ears."

"I thought I heard Brooke tell Annie she shouldn't have taken her diaper off because it was making the new couch wet."

"We'd better hurry and finish."

Knowing that laughter is the best medicine, I figure if we play the tape once a day, we'll never get sick. And when the offspring are finally grown and living elsewhere, we'll still be healthy enough to have our long, romantic interludes and, who knows, maybe we'll even sizzle.

CHAPTER 13

IN DISGUISE

Gee, I've read through at least a dozen or so "buying a car" guidebooks and I don't remember seeing anything about needing a pair of XY chromosomes as a pre-purchase requirement.

So it came as a bit of a surprise this morning at a car dealership when four salesmen sat around shooting the breeze as I, along with my two young daughters, walked around and around and around the same vehicle — I was even holding the brochure describing this particular car, which I thought to a salesman would be like waving a red flag in front of a bull.

But these "bulls" just weren't interested. In me, anyway. No, I can't say they were being openly rude and insensitive, I just don't think it dawned on them that a potential customer could actually be disguised as a woman with two preschoolers — so why bother?

Trying to decide if I should say something (that is, if I could somehow manage to get their attention), my temper kicked into gear when I noticed one of the "bulls" eagerly greeting a man who had just walked in.

But it wasn't until the rest of them stampeded over to him that I got really steamed.

Taking a couple of deep breaths to calm down (plus, I was a little dizzy from doing all that car circling), I knew the feminist in me would never forgive myself if I simply accepted the situation and walked away. Besides, my girls were with me; I just had to rise to the occasion as a "role model" for them. With Helen Reddy's "I am woman, hear me roar" roaring in my head, I marched over, ready for a showdown.

After getting their attention by innocently asking if the contents of a dirty diaper could be easily removed from the luxury sedan in the corner, I told them that while I had remembered my checkbook, my credit cards (in my name) and quite a bit of cash, I had somehow forgotten to bring my penis. And wasn't it a shame that that omission was obviously going to keep one of them from writing an order for me right then and there.

They stared. A couple of 'em bolted out to the car lot — they must have thought I was Lorena Bobbitt looking for a replacement part. Finally, one of them (and that's a start) "took his blinders off," broke into a huge grin and offered to show me the latest inventory.

Well, at least that's one salesman that's smart enough (now) to know that while people may not have the same "hood ornaments," he's got to look past their "front ends" and treat them all as potential customers.

I feld mildly triumphant, although I'm not sure the girls noticed. Still, if I don't batter away at those old discriminations, they'll still be around when my daughters go buy their computerized interplanetary vehicles.

CHAPTER 14

TODDLING AFTER FASHION

They say you shouldn't judge a book by its cover and I say, in addition to that, you shouldn't judge a mother by the clothes her two-year-old is wearing.

You see, we mothers of two-year-olds have no control over what these little tyrants choose to adorn themselves.

Oh, sure, we try. I can't tell you the number of cute little summer dresses accessorized with adorable bloomers and darling hair bows that sit on their original hangers in my daughter's closet with the original paper stuffing still intact in all their little sleeves in my daughter's closet.

But I can tell you the number of hours (over a million) I've spent reasoning (ever tried to reason with a two-year-old?), cajoling, whining, and yes, I'm not proud of it, begging this miniature tower of absolute stubbornness to please wear the outfit Daddy and Mommy have worked so hard to buy (guilt doesn't work either).

No more. Life's too short. All that's left to try are

"time-outs" and I have to save those for the really important things (like when she decides our pet needs a little accessorizing and uses one of my treasured miracle bras because the cups fit nicely over the dog's ears).

So now she chooses her own daily wear. For one of our frequent hangouts, the local bookstore, my pint-sized statement of style favors the "layered look": a ripped, faded purple leotard (I keep throwing it out, she keeps finding it it), followed by her most cherished, permanently Kool-Aid pink-stained sundress whose sunflower center has long since been ripped off and only a few, straggling pieces of yarn remain (I keep throwing it out, she keeps finding it). Completing her ensemble is a pair of "neutral" hot pink socks serving to highlight her glow-in-the-dark, neon green Minnie Mouse ballet shoes. You know, I've recently noticed that no matter what subject area I request the location of from one of those roving, bookfinder employees, my daughter and I, carefully following their directions, always end up in the "dress for success" section. A coincidence? I think not.

Regardless, I am beginning to get used to and even admire the flamboyant style my daughter is displaying. In fact, the other night I was feeling downright grateful for Annie's eclectic look. In the midst of an intense thunderstorm, we found ourselves suddenly plunged into total darkness. Closing my eyes in exasperation because my husband was traveling and he alone knew where the flashlight and matches were kept, I pictured the girls and I stumbling through the house in search of something that would give us light.

Then I opened my eyes and knew we would be just fine. Minnie Mouse, via Annie, had come to our rescue. I was amazed at the amount of illumination given off by two toddler-sized, glow-in-the-dark, neon green Minnie Mouse ballet shoes.

To me, they are the most beautiful shoes in the world.

SYLVIA
by Nicole Hollander
When Moms Get their own Fairy God-Mothers.
I KNOW YOU FEEL SURE THAT YOUR CHILDREN WILL BE TRACKING MUD AND SAND INTO THE HOUSE WHEN THEY'RE THIRTY.
I'LL NEVER BE ABLE TO TAKE A BATH WITH THE DOOR CLOSED.
MA!
nicole Hollander
4-1
©1995 BY NICOLE HOLLANDER
SOMEDAY YOUR CHILDREN WILL TAKE YOU OUT TO LUNCH AT A FRENCH RESTAURANT AND ORDER ESCARGOT.
DON'T TOY WITH ME.
MA, SHE'S LOOKING AT ME FUNNY.
AM NOT!

CHAPTER 15

NEVER LOOK A GIFT CRAB IN THE MOUTH

A word to the wise. Be wary, somewhat suspicious, *extremely* cautious when someone surprises you with a no-money-down, put away your checkbook, *absolutely* free...pet. Even if you happen to be looking for one at the time.

I always figured with two preschoolers, I would have many good years before the oldest decided a pet was in order. Maybe even a couple of decades if I was really lucky. Imagine my surprise when Brooke, upon her fifth birthday, announced she was ready to love, comfort and take care of a pet all on her own.

Needing some time to get used to the idea of an addition to the family, I suggested she practice on her little sister for, oh, say, a year or so. She could bathe Annie, feed Annie (who, as fate would have it, already enjoyed finding and eating from dog/cat dishes anytime we happened to be visiting someone with a significant furry other). Heck, I told Brooke she could probably even teach Annie to bark by making her think it was just another new word to learn.

But Brooke wasn't buying it. She saw nothing fun about having a pet she was genetically related to. And after a week of listening to her chant (even in her sleep): "If I don't get a pet I'll just die" (five-year-olds are known to be quite dramatic, especially when chanting), I began my own chant: "If she doesn't stop chanting soon, I'll just die" (thirty-three-year-olds can be equally dramatic). I knew the time had come to search for a low-maintenance, nonshedding sidekick for my daughter.

The next morning, just as we were beginning our pilgrimage to a pet store, I heard a knock at the door. It turned out to be Brooke's teacher, who, on a whim, stopped by to see if we might be interested in adopting one of the school's hermit tree crabs now that summer had arrived.

Mere coincidence that Mrs. Mollinghoff had brought, as a gift, exactly what we were going in search of? No way! I took this as a sign from God that we were meant to love, comfort and take care of this tiny crustacean. This tiny *free* crustacean.

After a nice chat, Brooke's teacher wished us well and went on her way. My five-year-old was in seventh heaven and asked if we could still visit the pet store to see if they had a book on hermit tree crabs. Feeling truly blessed at this recent turn of events because I figured I had saved quite a bit of money on the cost of a pet, I eagerly agreed that a trip to the store was still in order — after all, how much could one tiny book on hermit tree crabs cost?

Plenty.

Say, $97.23 to be exact. Well, actually, the book rang in at $2.50 but as soon as one of the ever-helpful salespeople saw me pick it up, he raced over and asked if we had purchased our hermit tree crab yet. Feeling *smug* because we already had our FREE crab, I smiled and sweetly said, "Thank you very much, but we are all set."

The salesperson then turned to Brooke and asked her what she had named her new friend. "Shelly," she replied. "Shelly," he sighed, "What a wonderful name. Gee, I bet Shelly really likes living in her terrarium with a vented cover and spends most of her days walking in the gravel, sand, or bark chips covering the bottom as she gets her very important exercise on the cholla wood placed lovingly in the center of the terrarium. And I bet you give her a choice, as all hermit tree crabs should have, between crab cakes and crab meal along with the special crab sponge filled with water, sitting in the corner on a piece of brightly colored coral shaped into a perfect water dish to sip from whenever she gets thirsty...," he continued. Listening to him, watching my daughter get teary eyed at the thought that we were denying her poor Shelly, I wondered if the hermit tree crab book was heavy enough to knock this guy out. Oh, well. Surely, he couldn't have much more to say.

Ha!

He completed his dissertation on every hermit tree

crab product known to humankind by sharing with my daughter the importance of having not one, not two, but as a bare minimum, three shells for her little buddy to move into, as he would continue to outgrow his seashell home anywhere from one to who knows how many times each year. At that point, I asked, SPECIFICALLY, how big her "little buddy" was going to get. Not to worry, he chuckled. All of the hermit tree crabs he had ever been around had remained small.

Twenty minutes later, at the checkout stand, dazed, surrounded by bags and bags of hermit tree crab accessories, I found myself writing a check for an amount greater than what I normally spend on groceries for a family of four in an entire week. Oh, and did I forget to mention that Shelly now had two new friends, as everyone knows (except me) that hermit tree crabs are quite social and thrive on company? Muttering about the fact that I could not believe I was spending so much money on a bunch of crabs, the checkout girl stopped what she was doing, looked deeply into my eyes and told me (in all seriousness) that even though it appeared to be a rather large sum of money, it was being well spent, as hermit tree crabs make wonderful pets. "Oh sure," I said sarcastically, "I'm sure my family and I will spend many hours of quality time watching them."

I should have kept my mouth shut because it is true what they say about ignorance being bliss. "Oh no," she said, "you don't just watch hermit tree crabs, you get to take them out three (*three!*) times a week for their baths." "Their baths?" I said in dismay. "Oh sure," she replied, "for cleanliness, improved respiration and additional body moisture, you need to submerge them in lukewarm water and after several dunks, allow them to air-dry."

And I knew who, after the novelty wore off, say, in a day or two, would be bathing these little aquatic animals three times a week.

Later that night, listening to me lament about how expensive this "free" pet had turned out to be and how I would have to bathe it and its buddies frequently (they do, by the way, have pincers), my husband, trying to cheer me up, said at least they were small and if they did pinch me, chances were really good it would not break the skin. He then turned on the news and we both stared in disbelief as a reporter was busy giving a rundown on a local fair and some of the more unusual items that could be purchased at the various booths. It wasn't what she was saying that caught our undivided attention — it was what was in the booth behind her.

There was a man holding — it took both hands — a very large hermit tree crab with a very large pincer. The reporter asked the man to say a few words and he mentioned that not only could these "lovable" creatures grow to a significant size, they were also quite durable and often lived well into their teens...

I can picture it now. In the not too distant future, not only will I get to deal with two female "human" teenagers, I will also be busy attempting to bathe three, probably gargantuan, hermit tree crab teenagers.

What next?

SYLVIA **by Nicole Hollander**

CHAPTER 16

MY FANTASY DINNER

We all have our fantasies and, oh, how mine have changed with the additions of my two children (three years old and seventeen months old). Here's my old fantasy: Having just finished a sumptuous meal at a really ritzy restaurant, my husband and I eagerly await the arrival of our chocolate mousse topped with tons of extra creamy whipped cream. In fact, we have the waiter bring the can of extra creamy whipped cream just in case we need more.

Suddenly, as though we've been magically transported, we find ourselves under the table with the can of, yes, extra creamy whipped cream and I'm pretty sure you can guess the rest...

Okay, here's my new fantasy: I find myself in a ritzy restaurant eating all alone. The kids are at home and Dad is babysitting.

I'm sure to those of you who often eat alone and especially to those of you who do not have young children, my new fantasy may sound a little bizarre and perhaps a bit sad or even boring. But let me share my reasons and I think you'll get the picture...

First and foremost, I would love to sit through a meal where I don't get food thrown at me. Do you know what it's like to have your sister and her new boyfriend surprise you with a visit and all the while she's there, she keeps staring intently at you and rubbing her hair (you immediately think she's got fleas or lice and quickly look at her new boyfriend to see if he's the carrier). They leave, and a few hours later you get a phone call asking how could you, I mean how could you, have embarrassed her like that??? It's then that she tells you about the big glob of toddler spaghetti mush that has somehow attached itself to the side of your head, firmly bonding with your strands of hair to display itself in some sort of Italian braid. Or better yet, how would you like to have pudding come flying your way to make an abrupt landing on the hair you have just had newly permed and are not supposed to wash for at least 48 hours?

Secondly, I would be ecstatic to get through one meal where I don't have to share any of my utensils or my drink with anyone else at the table. For some strange reason, my oldest feels she must use my fork or her food doesn't taste "right." The scenario goes like this: she drops her own fork, I pick it up, get her another one from the drawer. She drops her fork. I leave it on the floor and get another one from the drawer. She drops her fork. I leave it on the floor and in total resignation, give her mine. Magically, her fingers bond with my fork and she manages to hang onto it for the remainder of the meal. I end up trying to cut my own food with a spoon and knife (there are no more clean forks in the drawer) and after dinner, I end up stepping on the forgotten "dropped" forks on the floor...

Oh, and my drink? Well, even though I give my seventeen-month-old her very own "sippy" cup, she feels compelled to drink from my glass. Now, I don't think I'm a selfish person and normally I wouldn't mind sharing my drink with her, but when she takes a sip she leaves something in return. You see, she insists on sticking her entire tongue into my drink and so, whatever bits of food and God knows what else happen to be on her tongue at the time of the sip are then deposited into my glass for my very own drinking and viewing pleasure.

Finally, I would love to sit down to dinner and focus on one thing and one thing only: enjoying my meal. I can't understand why, when we've been together most of the day, my three-year-old decides at the dinner table to begin asking me all of the questions of the universe. I pour her milk, she wants to know how they make sure the milk is clean before we drink it. I serve her baked potato, she wants to know why potatoes come in the shape they do and why they don't grow on vines, like grapes do. I serve her the chicken, she wants to know where the feathers and beak are. She hears a plane overhead and wants to know how they fly since their wings don't flap like a bird's...and on and on we go...

Got the picture?

SYLVIA
by Nicole Hollander
When Moms Get their own Fairy God-Mothers.
I KNOW YOU'RE CONVINCED THAT YOUR SON WILL BE MAKING GROSS JOKES FOREVER AND GROW UP TO BE RUSH LIMBAUGH.
MA, WHERE ARE YOU?
IT'S HOPELESS.
nicole Hollander
4-26
LOOK AT ME! SOMEDAY YOUR SON WILL BE WITTY AND AMUSING AND YOU'LL BE ABLE TO INTRODUCE HIM TO PEOPLE OUTSIDE THE FAMILY.
MA, WHERE'S MY STUFF?
NO GIRL WILL MARRY HIM... HE'LL LIVE HERE FOR-EVER.

CHAPTER 17

A BITE OF THE AMERICAN DREAM

The good news is my two-year-old made a great impression on a new playmate. The bad news is the impression consists of my daughter's four molars, two canines and eight incisors.

Fortunately, the victim's father was quite gracious — no skin broken, no harm done (he even mentioned that it looked like Annie's teeth were all in perfect alignment). However, when he gently chided me on the importance of stopping such behavior early, so that I wouldn't end up with one of those "rough and tumble" girls, a "tomboy" if you will, I didn't feel so gracious in return.

For one thing, I'm not aware of any scientific studies that show a definitive relationship between being a tomboy and having a propensity toward biting. My friend Susan told me her three-year-old daughter (who has, since birth, refused to wear anything but dresses and enjoys hearing excerpts from "Miss Manners" as her bedtime story) recently decided to take a nice-sized chunk out of her father's leg just as he was telling her little girls were, indeed, made of "sugar and spice and everything nice."

But even more importantly, what's wrong with being a "rough and tumble" female? Gee, "yours truly" spent the majority of her childhood in cutoffs and t-shirts, was always the first or second "pick" for any of the neighborhood football games and had the distinction of being the local expert when it came to catching frogs, beetles and small, garden-variety-type snakes.

And I didn't turn out too badly. In fact, I have been a nonbiting (even viewing "Wolf" starring a furry Jack Nicholson didn't tempt me), law-abiding citizen for quite some time despite my early years engaged in less than "ladylike" behavior.

Sure, my daughter will be taught that it's bad manners to go around biting people (after all, you never know where they've been).

But she'll also be taught that trying to fit into one mold of what a "socially acceptable" female should be is not only an outdated pursuit, but can, in fact, keep her from realizing her potential.

You know, it's a pretty rough-and-tumble kind of world. Maybe that's why I think it's so important that Annie and all the other little girls out there grow up feeling in charge of their own destinies. And whether they choose to be in Shirley Temple frills tap dancing to "Goodship Lollipop" or faded jeans and one of their mother's old t-shirts digging for worms to use as fishing bait, they alone are responsible for garnering their own, great big bite of the American dream instead of waiting oh-so-patiently for someone else to bring them the "leftovers."

CHAPTER 18

LONELY TRIPS TO THE BATHROOM

I'm beginning to feel like I'm starring in my own "Groundhog's Day" movie everytime I'm asked about my family. The script goes something like this: "Do you have children?" "Yes, I have two little girls." "Hmmm, two little girls ... are you planning on one more in the hopes that it will be a boy for your husband?" I usually just smile (actually more of a grimace), remember what my mom always says about considering the source and go on about my business. But I'm really starting to think I need to try a different type of response because this just keeps happening again and again and again.

So what's the correct reply? "What does my husband need a boy for?"

It can't be sports, because I can't think of one sport that my daughters wouldn't be able to participate in due to their gender. Soccer, tennis, volleyball, track and field, swimming, football, basketball and even baseball

— to name just a few available to our girls. And the speed and accuracy the oldest is showing when she pitches to her ol' dad makes us think we just might have the next Nolan Ryan in the making.

It can't be to carry on the family name, because women changing their last names to match their mates' is getting less and less common. And many of those who do simply add his last name to the end of theirs. For example, can anyone say "Hillary Rodham Clinton?"

"Of course I'll give him a son — every man needs a fishing partner," but it just so happens that our four-year-old "princess" loves to fish, can in fact, sit patiently for hours on end (catching some nice-sized bass) while watching her dad and grandfather fidgit around with all of their nifty, new, and hopelessly tangled doodads. And while two of them might not like to admit this, if someone were to ask who had caught the most fish between the three of them, I'm afraid the little princess would come out way ahead of her fishing buddies.

My poor husband will, tragically, have to miss out on those incredibly bonding experiences of taking "gotta touch everything" toddlers to a public bathroom. But don't be concerned because he's assured me (usually every time I come back from the bathroom with the little darlings looking like I've been through a war zone) that missing out on that one aspect of being a dad is just fine with him!

So maybe that's it. Maybe that's the new response I'll give. The next time someone asks if I'm going to try again for a son, I'll just reply that no, my husband feels completely satisfied as as a father of two girls even though it means he has to go to the bathroom all by himself.

by Nicole Hollander

CHAPTER 19

A MOTHER'S RESUMÉ

In an earlier life, B.C. (Before Children), I was both a technical writer and a computer programmer for a large corporation. Going to the office each weekday was a joy, as I found my job challenging and satisfying. In addition, I worked with a great group of people and my various managers were constantly praising group of people and my various managers were constantly praising either verbally or in the form of bonuses, my contributions to the company. Oh, and three weeks of vacation along with five personal holidays (all to be taken at my discretion) was pretty easy to live with too...

Then my husband and I decided we would like to have a child. My pregnancy was a breeze. I continued to work at full steam ahead right up until the first labor pains. The day after Brooke was born, I found myself in a room filled to overflowing with flowers and gifts, the majority from well-wishing and extremely supportive co-workers.

Brooke and I headed home and four months into a

six-month maternity leave, I knew I would have to make the decision soon to return to the corporate world or make a significant career change and become a stay-at-home mom. Feeling fortunate at having a choice and wanting to make the best decision for me and my child, I figured a trip to the bookstore was necessary. I was in search of a books that would give me much needed insight into what being a stay-at-home mom would entail — a job description, if you will. Unfortunately, although I found numerous books that discussed everything else related to children and parents, there was not one (one!) book available that actually discussed what it was really like to be a full-time parent.

And now, after two years of being at home with Brooke, I understand why. For one thing, if the job of a stay-at-home mom was described in great detail, you would need to be a weightlifter to get the book off the shelf and a wheelbarrow to get it out of the car. Plus, if you started reading it when your child was a newborn, by the time you finally managed to get to the last page, that same newborn would be asking to borrow the car keys for the senior prom.

Nonetheless, I still believe it is important to publicize the lifestyle of a full-time parent. Not wanting to limit the buyers of my book to either weight lifters or people who never go to the bookstore without their wheelbarrows, I have decided to highlight just a few aspects of what I consider to be the most important job in the world.

Work Schedule:

Well, the good news is that there is no set work schedule. No predetermined, inflexible number of hours that you must clock in on a timecard. However, there is a catch to all this flexibility, and that is the bad news. You see, with the full-time parent career, there is no begin time and end time assigned to your job each day. To demonstrate this concept more fully with an example: if you have seen the "Never Ending Story," think of it like that, only this is titled "The Never Ending Job." Morning duty is followed by afternoon duty is followed by evening duty is followed by late night duty is followed by wee hours of the morning duty...

Job Duties:

I am a pharmacist. So much of the time, my child, who has been blessed with my allergies, is constantly on a series of medications at any one time. Not only do I have to remember the dosage and the number of times the medicine is administered, I must be aware of each medicine's side effect, not to mention which over-the-counter medications can be taken in sync with prescription medicines and if using both types, how one could affect the other mainly in terms of effectiveness. When I go to the pharmacy, I talk the talk and walk the walk and fortunately, I have a pharmacist who recognizes my growing expertise in the field and often says I should get my license.

I am an architect. I have designed and built a cathedral out of popsicle sticks that would rival Notre Dame. I have created an entire log cabin village in a single afternoon using only twigs, grass and glue. I understand the importance of building a solid structure which is defined as being able to withstand the incredible forces of a two-year-old. You know, I bet if my definition of a solid structure was made into an industry standard, dwellings of any kind would certainly last forever.

I am an engineer. When I used to get on an escalator, all I had to do was be ready to take the step off at the end of my ride so as not to be caught in the last folding stair. But now, with a toddler at my side, escalator riding has become much more complex. Now I am forced to understand completely the inner workings of the escalator (a lifting machine that makes use of pulleys and counterweights — a drive wheel moves a chain attached to the stairs while the returning stairs act as a counterweight) *and* be able to explain the description above to a two-year-old (snap your fingers once and it will give you an idea of their attention span) who must know how it works. Think for a minute: think about all the things you do during the day (make coffee, drive your car, wash/dry clothes, take a bath or shower, etc.) and what it would be like if you had an extremely insistent miniature human being that demanded to know how everything worked!

I am a chef. Sure, I am impressed with the likes of Julia Child and Martha Stewart. But, when you think about it, they very seldom prepare food for the same group of people, over and over again. In addition, the people they prepare their wondrous dishes for encourage variety and would most definitely cringe at the thought of being served the same type of food two days in a row, much less two meals in a row. So, as a result, I am much more impressed with the person who can come up with fifty ways to use peanut butter and jelly when faced with a toddler who decides those two ingredients must be used in every meal for months (and months) on end and (this is the catch) demands the presentation of those two ingredients be different each time. Take on that challenge, Julia or Martha!

I am a time management expert. There is an old wives' tale about women in my current career eating bonbons while using the remote control to click between the various talk shows and soap operas. Well, here is a hint to help clear up that misconception. The next time you are in the house of a mom who is with her child all day, every day, and take a close look at the box of bonbons on the coffee table. The outside wrapper is still securely attached to the candy box, is it not? Oh, and the remote control? Bet it has a bunch of dust and cobwebs on it from lack of use. The fact is, our days are spent either running after our little loved ones, or running around town to get them to whatever extracurricular activity we thought would enrich their lives. And if you are wondering what we do during nap time, that is when we become sanitation workers and launderers and seamstresses and financial wizards trying to balance a checkbook filled with unexpected child-related expenditures and so on and so on.

Compensation:

Well, if money, prestige and tons of recognition are important to you, this is going to be a dramatic change. There is no salary, there are no vacation days or personal holidays and more often than not, there will be limited support within the community regarding the legitimacy of your job. (At most check-out counters I am still viewed with suspicion when I say, "Yes, you heard me correctly. I do not have a work phone number.") And as for the business world, choosing to stay at home with my child was not a popular decision. Remember all that previous support from my beloved office buddies? Well, it disappeared from my life when I disappeared from the office.

So why do it? Why pick the hardest job in the world when there will be little, if any, of the traditional rewards coming my way? The answer is easy: I could not think of anything more challenging and satisfying than accepting the full-time responsibility for molding a tiny newborn into a contributing and caring member of society. And, as if that were not enough, I also have the added benefit of being the recipient of constant displays of affection and, believe me, all those hugs and kisses are worth their weight in gold.

Classifieds

Employment Section

Be Your Own Boss!

Become a Mom

18 YEARS OF GUARANTEED JOB SECURITY!

7-DAY WORK WEEK!

NO DOWNTIME!

(Standard 24-hour shift)

QUALIFICATIONS

Architectural Skills

Demonstrate ability to design/build cathedrals out of popsicle sticks and log cabin villages utilizing twigs, grass, and glue in one afternoon

Pharmaceutical Skills

Demonstrate thorough knowledge of all pediatric-related medicines and be willing to perform exhaustive studies on each medication's effectiveness

Engineering Skills

Demonstrate thorough knowledge of inner workings of sinks, toilets, coffee makers, cars, airplanes, escalators, elevators, automatic doors at Target, washers, dryers, etc., infinity, and be able to explain those inner workings in an effective manner to a very curious two-year-old

Cooking Skills

Demonstrate ability to prepare and present peanut butter and jelly in a minimum of fifty different ways

Time Management Skills

Demonstrate ability to be at two, three, four, pladces at one time and be willing to dedicate any free time (all five minutes of it) to sanitation-related activities

Financial Skills

Demonstrate the financial wizardry necessary to maintain enough of a balance in the checkbook for all of the unexpected child-related expenditures

Religious Skills

Thrive in the state of martyrdom with a lifetime goal of sainthood

Non-traditional package does *not* include:

Paychecks; Paid On-The-Job Training; Medical/ Dental Plan; Paid Vacation Time; Paid Sick Days; Bonuses or Advancement Opportunities, *but does include*: Satisfaction of raising caring individuals who will become contributing members of society AND infinite number of wet, sloppy kisses and bear hugs, which to a mom are worth their weight in gold.